Reminisce

CreateSpace Corporate Office
4900 Lacross Road (Mall Drive)
North Charleston, SC 29406
www.createspace.com

ISBN 978-0692453599

Printed in the United States of America

INTRODUCTION:

A Guiding Poet Revealed

I have had the pleasure of knowing Mr. Jim Mills for a few wonderful years. He is a dear friend with a wonderful personality and is highly spiritual. His kind words and gentle encouragement has made me grow as a poet and a human being. He was a guiding force in one of the lowest points of my life, and I can honestly say, that had he not been there for me, to lift my spirits, and encourage me to continue writing poetry, I may not be the poet I am today.

I have had the wonderful experience of seeing how his poetry uplifts the spirits of others. A very dear friend was being tormented by thoughts of something she did that she felt was wrong. She happened to read a poem entitled; "What's Your Decision?" It affected her deeply, for she had lost her spirit and felt as though she was not worth redemption. Reading Jim's lovely poem, gave her the forgiveness she sought, and strengthen her spirit. This is the magic and beauty of Jim's poetry.

In another situation, a young girl's intent on doing herself harm was talked out of her self-destruction, with Jim's loving and gentle advise. He wrote a poem for her that let her see the beautiful person that he saw. His lovely poem enabled her to believe in herself, and his encouragement led her to become one of the finest poets I have ever read. These incidents just reveal the beauty of a wonderful person and friend that Jim is to all who are lucky enough to become his friend. I believe no finer friend or poet could ever be found.

Jim's poetry is so honest and refreshing; its gentle beauty lifts one's spirit and refreshes the soul. His words of faith guide you lovingly into his world of a forgiving and patient God who is waiting for his children to see his glowing light and return to a well-trod path. There have been many times, when my spirit was low, and reading his beautiful poems have refreshed me, and given me the strength to carry on and see light at the end of the tunnel.

His poetry is heartwarming, intelligently written and expressed from the heart of a wonderful man. His keen insight into the feelings and emotions of others is expressed in many of his outstanding poems. His outstanding talent to express many of the experiences we often keep to ourselves awes me. He writes eloquently of love, sorrow, pain, and heartbreak. He manages to pull the reader into his lovely world... A world you do not want to leave any time soon!

Retta McKenzie
(Reindeer)
2003

TO WHOM THIS BOOK IS DEDICATED

This book is dedicated to all my
family and friends who believed in me
and influenced me in publishing a book of my work.

ACKNOWLEDGEMENTS

First, I must thank God for the gift He has given me. If it weren't for Him, I wouldn't be here and as successful as I am today. You will notice that His name is referenced throughout this book. I just can't imagine receiving such a wonderful gift and not showing any acknowledgement to the giver. I have knocked on His door, He opened it and truly blessed me with the wonders inside. He blessed me with a sense of empathy and communication skills in writing to share my testimonials in an effort to provide my perspective on life. For this gift, I pray that I use it the way He planned. God--thank you again for this lovely gift.

I would also like to give much thanks to the love of my life, Michelle Currin-Mills. God has blessed me with her, who is my driving force and true angel. She is the reason why I continued writing. She gave me that extra push needed with her inspiration and commitment to my overall happiness and success. It is such a blessing seeing her beautiful smile as she reads my poetry. Her love for my poetry gave me the strength needed to get this done. Thank you Michelle for molding and shaping me into the quality man that I am today and for our beautiful daughter, Mia!

I also appreciate my family for all the love and support they have given me throughout the years. When it came to my poetry, they've always provided me with good and honest feedback. They would read my work and ask the question, "Why aren't you published yet?" Those words of motivation gave me the drive needed to make my first book of poetry a reality. Thank you family for recognizing my talents and being an integral part of my motivation in the publishing of my work.

Last, I would like to thank all my friends who have provided me with the feedback that I also needed to boost my confidence in publishing. There are too many to name, but if I have forgotten to mention your name please forgive me. I must thank Michelle Best, Andrea Hampton, Rosette Carter, Angella Yap, Crystal, Francis Mobley, Audrie, Rex King, Angelia Udechukwu, Carissa Twitchell, Linda Hill, B. Thomas Daniels, and Retta (Reindeer) Mckenzie for their great and immediate feedback to all my works that I've posted on different sites.

Your feedback was very helpful and contributed to the depth, brevity and diversity of my poetry. Thanks for being there when I needed your views and thanks for caring about my success. Again; if I've forgotten anyone, please forgive me. I'd also like to give special thanks to Reindeer, who contributed to the great reputation that I have today by ensuring I was exposed to numerous authors in order to get their views of my work as another means of building my confidence. I also thank her for the collaborations which you will see in the book. In addition, I want to give special thanks to Carissa for writing that excellent poem for me that brought out many emotions. An extra special thanks goes to Thomas Hundley for assisting me with the publishing of my work. I truly believe that one of God's purposes for him was to pave the way for me. Thank you so much my brother! Last, I would like to thank those who have displayed my poetry in various programs in support of deployed Service Members, graduations and history month observances. I was deeply honored to be able to support those great programs. – Jimmy "Jim" Mills

PREFACE

Remember...Never Forget

You the reader, now hold in your hands, one of the most beautiful and inspirational books of poetry that I have ever read. The wonderful poems in this book will soon fill you with joy and inspiration, sadness and tears, for they detail the life of one of the best men I have ever known. His lovely prose will get into your mind and heart and gently lift you to a place where few have ever been, in the arms of a loving God, and the soul of a true child of God.

There have been many days, when my spirit was weak and needed restoring. I found this need filled by the beautiful poems I read in Jim's Anthology. His lovely poems restored my faith in humanity and took me away from the thoughts that darkened my life. I was refreshed and led into a world where good truly overcomes evil and mankind finds forgiveness and redemption in the words of this fine poet.

I was truly astounded and awed by his ability to affect the lives of those who read his wonderful and spiritual poems. I have seen their affect first hand, in the troubled lives he touched, in the beauty of his spirit as he reached out to help those who needed his gentle words and kind heart.

His poetry is written with such honesty and purity of spirit, a rare thing in the troubled world we live in today. This is but one of the attributes that attracted me to Jim's work, for in his gifted words of prose, you find true joy and love, inspiration and hope. His heart is uncluttered by harshness or judgments and his glorious verses leap off the page and you find them embedded in your heart and mind bringing you a smile that such a rare beauty truly exists in the world.

I believe you will find Jim's poetry such a wonderful addition to your life, for you can return to read it as often as you need. It will make your day much brighter and beautiful as you turn each page and take a wonderful journey into the life of a true "Child of God."   --Retta (Reindeer) McKenzie

A Child of God

You, sir, are a child of God,
One of the greatest I know.
You are His gift to Earth.
A gift full of gentleness
And great strength.

God's path has tested you time and time again,
But I have a feeling you took on each challenge
And gave it your all to conquer it.
Each challenge most likely helped you to find
A new found strength inside yourself.
God may not have given you the straight & narrow path,
But He has used your path to make you the man you are today.

Any disappointing times or possible failures you've hidden inside,
But you also have this unseen beauty inside.
Truth is a trait that seems to be easily instilled in you.
Wisdom you seem to hold tucked away
For that certain time when you need it most.

You are one child of God
That's willing to listen while we talk
And do everything in your power to help.
God ever uses you to light up the world.
You truly are a work of art,
Especially when you lighten the day with a simple "hi".

You, sir, are a child of God
One of the greatest I know.
You're one amazing person
And I'm proud to call you, my friend.

04.08.2003 (For LC) --Carissa Twitchell

9

Reminisce

(Remembering the Past)

Jimmy C. Mills

CONTENTS

PART ONE: INSPIRATION   12

PART TWO: LOVE AND ROMANCE   29

PART THREE: UPLIFT   42

PART FOUR: HAIKU   58

PART ONE

-- -- -- -- -- -- --

Inspiration

(Food for your Soul)

Genesis

Dark clouds consumed all the lands
A new age is upon us
Raining seeds of evil everywhere
Keeping every man on their knees lifting their hands

An uncontrollable outbreak spreading in the east
Now the minds of man are tainted
Giving birth to an age of darkness and sin
Earthly bound idols are worshipped is the picture painted
Lord is a distant memory

Our lives in ruin ... everyone's in sorrow
Realizing we don't want to live for tomorrow

Or we can live within a white cloud
Understanding our actions can bring everlasting life
Reciting the good news out loud

Saving our souls and living as directed
Aiding in the genesis where
Victory is given to the believers
In their spread of the good news as they share
Overseas from country to country
Reliving Jesus in the minds of the receivers

Good things come to those who believe
Others will parish
Deliverance is behind the door ... knock

Lost Souls

Lost souls are becoming the ordinary
While fruitful minds become an endangered species
Because some souls are being influenced by shepherds
Leading flocks with false prophecies

Sewing bad seeds in rich soil
Causing confusion within weak minds
Using damaged tongues to contaminate
And hide superficial wisdom with blinds

As their souls lie dormant deep in dark woods
Listening to sounds of reptiles and snakes
Unleashing venoms of dark poison
To tear their hearts like earthquakes

As the harvest of deception grows
A vaccine can bring light to darkness
It contains sixty six ingredients
To nourish a lost soul with the fruit of life and happiness

Shadow

I am with you till the very end
Because you are my love and my best friend
I will always be there for you and will not slack
Like a shadow when you're facing east, I got your back

You can run but you cannot hide
I am part of you so I'll always be by your side
I'm there through your pain and your suffering
I'm empathetic with you so use me to do all your buffering

We are journeying through life together
And I'll cherish every moment of our life forever
when life is lost, I'll live under God's control
I am your soul

The Gift

Everyone was given a special gift
A gift that would uplift at least one spirit
During your lifetime
And all you have to do is use it

For the purposes in which He gave
It's one of His children He wishes you to save
Whether it be through laughter or excitement
Or through the fruit of enlightenment

He wants you to use your gift
To uplift someone's soul
Before the dark angel
Takes control

I know my gift
It's the gift of feeling and expression
What do you do
To deliver someone through depression?

Once I Acknowledged Him…

Once I acknowledged Him
I became a better man
A man who lived under God's plan
Giving my all to help others
For I view them all as my sisters and brothers

Once I acknowledged Him
I excelled in my careers
Becoming more successful
Meeting Godly peers
And becoming more useful

Once I acknowledged Him
I started looking deeper
My intelligence soared
Making God a keeper
Someone never to be ignored

Once I acknowledged Him
Goodness overshadowed the bad
I was weak and now I'm strong
Happy days come more than the sad
How can loving Him be wrong?

Whispers in the Wind

It's a perfect day today
It's dawn and the air is cool across the bay
Mesmerized by the clear reflection of the land and sky
This mirror image created a symmetry pleasing to the eye

As my naked feet paddled in the water, I unwind
While my arms balanced me from behind
My head faced the sky ... I'm blind
As the whispers of the wind blew my mind

Resonating with skill
I was hypnotized by the thrill
of nature's captivating sound
Of whistling winds and leaves hitting the ground

And waves flowing to shore
My ears tuned in wanting to hear more
As I heard tree leaves steadily swaying ahead
Sounding so peaceful as the Birds chirped over my head

While my feet were massaged by the warm waves, I felt fine
As the wind weaved through my hair, a chill ran down my spine
Ah....what an indescribable feeling
Leaving me weightless like I floated above earth's ceiling

So invigorating and pulsating, I had to embrace
My eyes released diamonds that fell down the sides of my face
I opened my eyes, gasped and exhaled slowly
Nervously feeling a presence that was with me solely

Viewing the sun in the shape of cross, I was at peace
It was calm, suddenly quiet and the wind began to cease
I got up, took off my veil and left the dock
Ready to do His bidding in the midst of His flock

My Faithful Journey

I want to go on a cruise
So which one do I choose
I have nothing to loose
But a ticket to use

I can cruise the ship called Ecstasy
Or the one called Faithful Journey
One's so inviting its where everyone wants to be
The other is so old it looks like it'll sink at sea

Ecstasy has a long line
Faithful Journey has only nine
A good decision lies deep in the mind
Then Faithful Journey shined

I followed my heart

Sounds of erosion echoed as it left the dock
Everyone on board was in complete shock
Many knelt down to pray
I followed suit and that's why I live today

Faithful Journey gave us a terrifying trip
A cruise I would've love to skip
As the unexpected hurricane gave rise to deadly waves
Had all of us viewing inside our graves

The storm was fierce and unyielding
And our togetherness was building
Prayer after prayer permeated everywhere
Terrified as hell…for each other, we were there

It was dark
Lightning was striking the seas
The waves consumed our ship
What a hell of a trip

Our ship was sinking and began to split
But our praying never quit
Then the storm ended and so did our fear
The sea became calm and land was near

Once we reached the land
We were informed that Ecstasy sank
Everyone died
We all cried

Truth

The truth is right before your eyes
Those who see and follow believe
Those who see and ignore are lost
Those who are in the valley can't even conceive

A farmer must plant seeds of understanding
To nourish the souls of the blind
While fertilizer is laid
To kill thorns of temptation in the weak mind

For the seeds that bare good fruit
Will quickly blossom in the light
But will lie dormant
In the darkest of night

Seeds of truth create vision
Vision is developed through prophecy
Prophecy reaffirms truth
The truth shall set you free

The Example

He provided the example many years ago
Guiding and showing us the way
So that you and I would know
How to live in this world today

That is blanketed by darkness
As bright lights beam through the cracks
Overshadowed and in duress
Light seekers are mere artifacts

Teachers of historical truth
Being displayed in shame
While closed blinds contain our youth
Who is to blame?

As they remain lost in muddy waters
Swimming in the wrong direction
Our poor sons and daughters
Clearly need resurrection

Then a bright light shined through the blinds
Shining brightly from the East
Brightening the most darkest minds
Tainted heavily by the beast

As the purest water
Flows through dark crevasses like veins
Changing wicked hearts
Into vessels of love linked by chains

Infectiously spreading from within
Blossoming like roses in rich soil
While weeds darken from roots of sin
As spirits are reclaimed and anointed with oil

Spirit

Souls
Pirating within your abyss
In search of
Realities beyond
Interpretation and
Time

Jesus

Just as He came
Everyone knew His name
Saving us from our sins
Until the very end
Salvation came to those who believe

Blessed

Better
Love
Every
Soul
Saved
Each
Day

Thank You! Thank You!

Thank you for my life for I owe my existence to yoU
Here I continue to exist cause I'm not on your list sO
As I kneel to pray, I'll give thanks for living another daY
Never forgetting what you've done that's why it's You I thanK
Kneeling with clinched hands asking how I can be a better maN
Youth was hard; always finding myself in a dilemmA
Over this and that. Thanks for carrying me thougH
Us together brings me courage to face giants without thoughT

Resurrection

Rallying here are thirteen men who
Entered a room to witness The Passover
Servants of God given bread and water
Used to covet Christ's body and blood
Reacting with curiosity because of Jesus' prophecy
Revealing that one will betray Him
Even deny Him prior to His
Crucifixion at The Skulls in front of thousands
Then Joseph set Jesus
Inside a Tomb of Stone
On the third day He was resurrected
Now we know He died for our sins

Reflections

Every day we see ourselves
Through a body of water, glass or a mirror
When we examine
Is it interior or exterior?

Do we see the truth
Or a body of lies?
Digging deep in the abyss
Will gather information like spies

We will then see what He sees
And will not be surprised at judgment
As our reflections display our truths
Providing opportunities for change and commitment

Because none of us live in a glass house
Hiding bones of sin underneath our skin
Reflecting to the masses what is good
While fighting inner demons and feeling chagrin

So as you see your inner truths
And your actions don't follow His command
You can take a turn down the right road at any time
So His Branch can extend to you His loving hand

What's Your Decision?

What is your decision?
Are you in or are you out?
I'm not trying to create tension
I'm just trying to get a feel for what you're all about

My judgment is coming so whose side are you on?
Are you with him or are you with me?
Make the right decision now before life is gone
What must I do to make you see?

I am the truth as I've consistently shown in the past
And he is a venomous snake who will deceive you
I am always with you and my love will forever last
While he'll leave and abandon you at any second to name a few

Your eternal life is very important to me
My loving child, make a decision before it's too late
And join my loving community
Where righteousness and justice prevails without hate

Your time has come to exude everlasting happiness
I know that you've veered off the path a time or two
But you know that I'm full of love and forgiveness
So what's your decision, I'm asking you?

Omega

Alpha came and there was light
He was pleased then darkness took flight
As His laws were ignored by the majority
And privilege only came to the seniority
Now very established in their own way
Many even forgotten how to pray
So there's no love for those in need
Because greed grew like a seed
As we worship idols we can see
Instead of the only true deity
A warning came to all in a Book of Sixty Six
If you're not in His club, you had better fix
Because judgment is coming our way
And no one really knows the day
So be prepared and stay the course
Because He will strike with an indescribable force
That will break through any barrier in its path
The most prominent cities will be leveled in His arm of wrath
As deep cracks tear into the ground from all ends
And twisters cause mass destruction as well as whirlwinds
The seas and fires engulf the land
People need to understand
No one survives
Judgment when it arrives
Everyone will lie on the ground
Motionless without sound
The seas will be red
Every flesh will be dead
Earth is no more
Forevermore

In that day, the chosen will rise and receive His blessings. Keep the
faith!

After

I hear cries, screams and pleads everywhere
A strong stench of charred ruins consumes the air
I open my eyes and to my surprise
What I'm seeing, I can't surmise

Holograms looking perplexed as they scan around
Viewing all the bodies laying on the ground
I also see total destruction blanketed by the night
With smoke lingering in the air and no moon in sight

I see strong leaders who are now begging for mercy
I see skyscrapers as rubble in the midst of a city
Wondering if we are hell bound
As I view myself motionless and lying on the ground

Then out of nowhere comes a loud trumpet sound
It doesn't appear that it's heard from all around
Then a very bright light slowly approaches out of the night
Why doesn't everyone see this beautiful sight?

Then a beautifully thunderous voice says, "Come to me"
My body became weightless, began to rise - could this be?
I also see other holograms rising toward the light
But many remain in the night

Oh my ... I'm finally a witness to His glory!
As He sits on His throne, this is no longer a story
With His son and a six winged angel near
I no longer have anything to fear

As we all prepare for the great feast
Away from the pressures of the beast
Life is the best it has ever been
Living within a wall without sin!

PART TWO

Love and Romance

(Words from the Heart)

What a Woman Really Wants

A man
A bread winner
One who takes care of home
One who does not roam

One who is sensitive and kind
One who is her unique find
One who consistently makes a scene
As he shows the world how to treat a queen

One who is loving and caring, but very tough
And when the lights go out, one who can get rough
And understands when she's had a hard day
As he uplifts her with a bouquet just because it's Wednesday

She wants a man with vision who thrives success
And never settles for anything less
A man with all of the above perfectly blended
And a man who understands that chivalry never ended

A man who lives by Ephesians 5
Because it's her happiness he thrives
He will know when her expectations have been met
When she can look him in the eye and just cry

This Ring

This ring represents a union
Of two souls compatible in every way
It is the bond that binds us together
And makes us whole till our dying day

This ring represents a merger established by God
A symbol of the strength that enhances our spirituality
It is a sign of stability which builds serenity
In God's community beyond the depths of our reality

This ring is a symbol of the promise
I extend to you as your faithful husband to be
One who will remain a Loyal confidant throughout our lives
Is it yes or no, will you marry me?

My Greatest Treasure

All my life, I've been in search of my greatest treasure
Traveling around the world just to find what I'm looking for
Through years of stumbling across what I thought would measure
I finally found what I truly adore

After maps lead me through paths of obstacles and dead ends
I realized that nothing goes as I plan
For it's His plan that guides me with the assistance of Godly friends
To nurture me from a young adult to a man

For my development was only a part in the His plan
The other was building my faith in Him to deliver my gift
Which He will deliver upon me becoming a man
As I matured, my life began to take a shift

Then I received His gift in the form of a spirit
Teaching me that true love is stronger from within
Souls merging into one so quickly one could only fear it
Our hearts grew stronger everyday leaving no room for sin

My greatest treasure is the His gift to me
She brings me so much happiness and love
My angel, shared spirit, and gift molded and shaped to be
My one and only true blessing sent from the Lord above

My Diamond

My diamond is my gem
A sparkling image of pure beauty
Delivered to me by yours truly
To make me the happiest man I could ever be

She shines every time I see her
Like a crystal's glittering light from the sun
She brightens at my very presence
Acknowledging to me that I'm her number one

Her true feelings were exposed
When puddles of joy formed in her pupils
As she described this overwhelming feeling
From unexplained experiences that could only be miracles

That eventually brought us together
Taking us both to another place
Her happiness truly showed
When I looked into her face

At that very moment
I knew that I was her best friend
As well as her diamond
Till the very end

My Rib

For years, I felt like a puzzle with a missing piece
Searching through life's labyrinth only to find dead ends
Trial after trial…moving me in the wrong direction
Making every reminisce a memory of a bad reflection

As I'm trapped in this net of emptiness and despair
My self-esteem plummeted into the deep…too much to bear
So I looked North for strength and deliverance
Years have passed but I was still in this circumstance

Then suddenly, destiny confronted me in the face
I finally felt like I was in the right place
Feeling more complete than ever before
What an abrupt heeling of this life-long sore

My missing piece is found ... is this what I am living for?
Is life's mystery revealing itself by opening its door?
Like a part of me was lost and now it's found
Perfectly intertwined we are truly bound

Like Adam, I felt alone in this land of plenty
Then His grace took a part of me to make my destiny
I was then filled with happiness
For my destiny delivered me from sadness

Roses with Meaning

The First Rose is dedicated to our creator who brought us together
The second is for our friendship that will last forever
The third forever binds our spirits into one
The fourth represents the births of our daughter and son

The fifth brings us luck in achieving our goals
The sixth brings internal strength to our living souls
The seventh symbolizes our closeness even when we're at a distance
The eighth represents our ability to persevere over any circumstance

The ninth signifies the joy that you bring to my life
The tenth represents the day you become my wife
The eleventh denotes the sadness that we will share between us two
The twelfth exemplifies my everlasting love for you

Reminisce

I am sitting on the beach
With my feet in the burning sands
My elbows relaxed on my knees
While my chin is cuffed in the palms of my hands

Looking at horizon's beauty
Of the clear blue sky and ocean view
Mesmerized by the sparkling crystals
As the ocean dissects the sun in two

Feeling relaxed from the soothing sound of waves
And the warmth of the massaging sand
My senses are stimulated by the wonders of nature
Causing me to reminisce on the day you gave me your hand

As I remember that beautiful dress and your lovely smile
Your hair masterfully done in the most elegant style
With that hourglass figure of a well crafted profile
makes every day with you seem so worthwhile

Like the day when I asked you the question
I will never forget the look of surprise on your face
Or the days spent on our numerous trips
The overwhelming joy you displayed took me to a place

That brings me back to the day we first met
Two lonely hearts in search of one another
The best day of my life
Was the day we finally found each other

My true companion ... my greatest gift
Missing you dearly every minute I'm away
So know that you're always in my thoughts
And that I pray for our reunion every day

Strength

It seems we're forever in the distance
Where galleries are our only comfort
Caused by two aspirations
Separating a union with another port

Year after year
Day after day
Visions of how things should be
Haunt me in every way

The constant pain is overwhelming
As the heart gradually will tear
Darkness overshadowing the light
The cold is too hard to bear

Then spawned strength from the deep
An unbreakable bond of the heart
Uplifting sacrifices into a future of hope
That kept us from being apart

The Anticipation

My heart pounds aggressively
As I gently caress the hair on her head
Thinking about the pure beauty of my Queen
As she lies exposed on the bed

Drenching with sweat all over her body
Screaming with all of her might
As she looks me in the eye
And clenches my skin so tight

With her legs up in the air
I continue to rise with anticipation
As the climax draws near
She pushes and pushes with frustration

The pain is so intense
Every second, I get more excited
And shake with anticipation
We have never been so united

As the head exits her body
She became more relaxed and screamed less
everything was calm
Then came, "My beautiful Princess!!!"

Tight Blue Jeans

A long day finally coming to a close
I'm walking behind her as we approach the door
My eyes are totally focused inside her clothes
My brain is focused on her inner core

Adrenaline is flowing indeed
As her assets move from side to side
I am truly a brother in desperate need
Of a long awaited ride

It's been months and I cannot wait
Tonight she's finally going to give in
I'm on the rise and she is my bait
It's about eight and I'm ready to begin

She's already wearing loose clothing
The candles are lit; slow music is playing and more
The anticipation is what I'm loathing
I'm salivating like a carnivore

She sits me down and then kisses me
States she's going to loosen up a bit
When the door closed, I stripped down to be ready
Wasting no time I must admit

My heart pumped faster as the door slowly opened
And to my surprise, I was in dismay
As she came out in tight blue jeans
Followed by my friends screaming HAPPY BIRTHDAY

Man.......my wife got me again.

A Mother's Love

No other love can compare
To a love of a mother I must say
It's unconditional in every way
And she'll be there for you till her dying day

Reaching outer limits for your success
As she disregards some of her deepest values for your happiness
Traveling long distances to render you aid
And always there to build your confidence when you're afraid

You are her number one
Whether you're her daughter or her son
She carried you for only nine months
But her umbilical cord remains connected to your soul

A bond that will never break
No matter how hard you shake
Make no mistake, she may be your worst
But when it comes to you or her, she'll put you first

Hidden
(Collaboration with Retta "Reindeer" Mckenzie)

I tried to conceal it, but I've been read and understood,
My secret's revealed for all to see,
To others its wrong, but to us it's nothing but good,
How I wish they would just let us be!

Our distance is misleading,
But our hearts are so close,
So to everyone I'm pleading,
Let me have this one thing I desire the most!

The cost of leaving this relationship is too hard to bear,
I will never find a love to equal this,
Our hearts are a matching pair,
Our love for each other is beyond compare…

So why do others stop and stare,
At this love they wish they had,
In our hearts we know the truth,
A love like this should not be hidden

PART THREE

- - - - - - - - - - - -

Uplift

(Words of Inspiration)

Determined

I see where I want to be
I know where I want to go
And no one can stop me
I'm determined…don't you know?

I received my diploma
That's not enough
I will matriculate through my Doctorate
No matter how tough
Because I'm determined

I will reach my goals
There's no hurdle too high
I am driven and will play my roles
Because I'll never position myself to only get by

I am determined to go the distance
I want to be an inspiration to others
Giving back in an instant
To my fellow sisters and brothers

The same applies to those I call friend
If you are determined…we can run this race
and carry each other till the very end
As long as you don't hinder my pace

No matter what the cost
I will persevere
I will not get lost
There's no need to fear

I am determined!

Unstoppable!

I'm in a sea of sharks
Trying to catch a single fish
Consistently challenged with barriers
But I'll get my wish

My position is clearly defined
So don't ever get in my way
I'm Poised with determination
You will address me as General someday

Displaying insurmountable leadership
No one can touch me
No officer can derail me
My clout is greater than any enemy

So continue to build barriers
Continue to tell me I'm done
I will continue to lift my hands and pray
For the day I'm your number one

When you look up to me for leadership
Ask me to advise
Seek me out for mentorship
My loyalty to you I'll never compromise

So please understand I'm unstoppable
You can't hold me behind bars
Like a Hawk, I'll break free and fly
Until I reach the stars

United

For years they were the symbol of financial strength
The objects of political power
Standing so tall they scraped the sky
As the clouds hide the top of each tower

Our melting pot's distinguished twins
Fell at the whip of the beast
Creating a smoke that clogged the veins of the city
And caused the loss of over 3,000 at least

Anticipated violent acts of sin
Shocked and united a nation in chagrin
Still mourning the loss of many
This spiritual war is about to begin

United as a nation, we hung our flags
And looked to the King for guidance
As we stretched our arm to the source of the whip
Knowing we can't win in this spiritual circumstance

With Him, we persevered
But like an Octopus, it has many tentacles
Spreading its arms around the world like a virus
As we became the world's vaccine and their obstacles

Spirit

I am a "pure breaded" southern woman
Strong in my faith ... strong in what I believe
Using my gifted voice and charisma
To lead millions in marches hoping to achieve

Civil rights ... for I'm the backbone
of my husband's greatest movement
As I stood by his side through all the tyranny
And the oppression is my testament

He is no longer with us
But I will never let his ideals lie
Dormant in our history ... for as long as I'm alive
His spirit will never die

Carrying his weight was no easy task
As I broadened focus to include world peace
Economic issues, women and LGBT rights
Praying that one day inequality and hatred will cease

I also published my memoirs, established the King Center
And fought for my husband's birthday to be federally recognized
All to keep his dream alive
and preserve his legacy to one day see his efforts realized

A Century ... Still Striving

The struggle continues
Will we ever rise above this segregated tower
It may appear that we have
But subliminally, we remain lesser to another power

Deeply rooted and unified for a single purpose
Amidst the calamity we were forced to endure
Standing together and marching for change
Hoping to one day find a cure

From years of protests, we gradually achieved successes
milestones met with incarceration or death
Still our leaders for change
Continue to strive till their last breath

Lifting our spirits and strengthening our resolve
To one day climb out of this abyss of segregation
Where different races come together
To unify as a nation

That understands we are all created equal
That we are stronger together
As the winds of tyranny left us off-balanced
Our shields of hope gave us direction and perseverance
To soon get what we were promised years ago
No matter the resistance

We will press on in another century
Striving, in one accord, to change this paradigm
Reaching all who care to listen
As we continue the efforts of those who sacrificed in this time

Style

I feel uplifted
Because I'm unique
The spotlight's on me
Who will critique?

My inimitable style
Builds my confidence
Poised with conviction
Is my conscience

Upright and sharply clad
Shining brightly in a dark room
Visibly seen by all
It's almost too much to consume

As I enter the room
Manicured and tailored to perfection
My heart pounds aggressively
As they begin their inspection

Of my hair design
Perfectly enhancing my features
And of my dress
As it accentuates my curves

I am a sight to see
Turning heads in the crowd
With a style of beauty
Standing tall and proud

Beauty

Beauty is in my eyes and that's no surprise
With a body and face so captivating it's enough to make any man rise
My poise is breath-taking, attractive and demands respect
So if you want in my space, you better come correct
Because I am beauty

When I hit the scene, the men can't help but adore
How I cat walk swiftly across the floor
As they stay tuned as if I'm live on a set
Giving them a show they will never forget
Because I am beauty

My hourglass figure is distinctive and a sight to see
Barbie ... you don't have nothing on me!
So sit back and watch as I draw the crowd
strutting my stuff ostentatiously and proud
Because I am beauty

My eyes are ebony and are perfectly blended with my skin
A true sister from within; I'm always confident and never chagrin
As my clothes perfectly fit this sexy and conservative figure
Like Mona Lisa, I make the picture
Because I am beauty

Armored

His armor is thickly plated
Impenetrable like titanium
His truth lies deep within
Soft as cotton and smooth like skin

The light can't shine through
Because the armor is woven into his body like fabric
So an angel was sent to penetrate
Steadily peeling through before it's too late

He is tall and dark like a tower
She is short and bright like a fairy
sowing seeds that grew seven branches
Through all the climbs and avalanches

Barriers were broken
Seams were filled
As the armor pierced, in came the light
And his blinders opened to a beautiful sight

Tears fell just moments before his time
And his angel came to fulfill her purpose
To help him pray for forgiveness of the days lost
Like the man who spoke to Jesus on the cross

Out of Time

If I could go back in time
I would relive this life changing mistake
That predetermined my destiny
With a sentence I cannot shake

Now I'm a walking time clock
With batteries that are low
Striving to make a monumental change
Before I have to go

Traveling all over the globe
Teaching the facts and being an inspiration
To those who share the same fate
In this virus stricken nation

I'll never let this fate ruin my life
Because my heart will never break or bend
I will remain strong
And fight this till the very end

Taken

I have a secret and it's still too hard to tell
At times I communicate with body language and other times I just yell
It all started when I was 12 years old and very naïve
With a situation so horrid, no parent could even conceive
After that experience, I secluded myself from the environment
Using firewalls stronger than walls concealing plans for the government
I didn't know where to turn or who to confide in
As I moped around feeling chagrin because I was forced to sin
I was stripped of my innocence without choice
Why couldn't they hear the screeching sounds of my voice?
I was too weak to break free
And now I'm another victim in this vicious society
Trying to end this seed of abhorrence inside of me
As I watched myself die and resurrect into someone I chose never to be
I feel so violated, unclean, and lonely
Because my innocence was taken without choice—can't you see?

Intense

Is that my daughter on the other end of the phone
Nervously crying while she screams for her life
Taking off as fast as I could to make it back home
Every stop light wasn't even seen along the way
Nervously I sweated as my heart beats faster and faster
Suddenly I drove into the garage and rushed into the house
Everyone yells, "Happy Birthday!"

Attraction

As I draw near
Tormented with fear
Trying to look inside
Ready for the prize
Acting like a man in the desert
Captivated by the site of an oasis
Trying to satisfy his every need
Injection operations indeed
Off goes the clothes!
Now where is she going?

Living in the Negative

Negativity rules!
364 I could be a stud
But the day I fall short, my name is mud
I just can't explain human behavior
Reaping you with praises when you're on target
But treating you like a disease when you're off the mark
To think that we're all human
And expected to be perfect…hmmmm..
And what about ourselves?
We barely give ourselves a break
As we dwell on a simple mistake
Losing all our faith and hope
We can't even cope
As we dwell on the past and lose self esteem
We begin to lose sight of our dream
Look at Job, Paul, Joseph, and Jeremiah
With all their trials, they still turned to our Messiah
And their days became much brighter
Because He showed them how to become a stronger fighter
As He can show you and me
So tell me … how should we really be?

Remembrance (Eagles to Doves)

All I can remember was that sweltering heat
The insurgents out there to defeat
And the last conversation with my wife
Giving me the greatest news of my life

She was pregnant with our first
Nothing could be worse
Than making the ultimate sacrifice
Lord knows that I'd do it twice

Because on that very day
I was proud to be a Screaming Eagle
Flying down to numerous objectives
To change the lives of this country's natives

So they can enjoy the freedoms we embrace
We didn't care what we had to face
We were there showing honor, courage, and commitment
A true Band of Brothers is my testament

We found numerous caches
We were integral in their successful election days
While capturing numerous insurgents
Which ensured the safety of the local residents

A long successful day was finally done
We were marching to our fortress to rest for another one
I was thinking to myself
We only have two months left

And then a cell phone rang.........

When I opened my eyes
I saw life for the very first time
Everything was bright and to my surprise

The feeling I felt was so sublime
As my weightless body lifted to the air
White wings extended and it was a shock
As I moved towards the sky all I could do was stare
Because I saw two of my friends flying in the flock

Of doves moving towards the sun
I heard the following words whispered in my ears
"Welcome home my son"
My eyes were full of tears

Proud

I am proud of those who make sacrifices for me
So I can live the American dream
To be all I can be
In a country where I can live free

Whether you are an Army of one
The few and the proud, a seaman,
Or the boys in blue
I want you to know that I'm proud of you

For sacrificing your lives and families
So I can enjoy life's pleasantries
From sea to shining sea
You bring freedom and peace to our loving country

Because of your courage and commitment to me
I am free and happy
For all the sacrifices you've made
I am deeply saddened for the losses paid

I am very proud of all the things you do for me
In distant lands all for the sake of our country
So I'll stand tall and salute you because I can
You make me proud to be an American!

PART FOUR

- - - - - - - - - - - -

Haiku

(Japanese Style; syllables 5 - 7 - 5)

The Curse

You come from within
You begin your life in sin
and cursed till the end

The Path

Can lead you astray
Depends on the turn you take
It's your decision

The Lone Wolf

You can hide for now
Later come out the closet
You'll still be lonely

The Truth

Brings you happiness
Takes away the hurt and guilt
It will set you free

Revelation

The script was written
We play our roles very well
End of Days is near

Faith

Everyone has it
Many don't believe in it
They will live in fear

Debt

You can't live with it
You can't survive without it
I stay deep in it

Why?

You take me away
You beat me then you kill me
I have to ask…why?

Tested

You will be tested
It may be your worst challenge
You're never ready

The Objective

I know the mission
I must develop some plans
To meet objectives

Explode

I'm nervous as hell
I'm strapped and ready to go
Got on the bus.....BOOM!

Wire

I hear everything
The honest truth will be told
Don't blow our cover!

Got Milk?

Watch out now fellas
They are growing up real fast
Now you are in jail

MADD

One more for the road
What happened? Can't remember
Someone died tonight

Satellite

I am working here
You are working over there
You're the satellite

The Thinker

He's not facing me
His chin is lying on his fist
What is he thinking?

Any Last Words?

The question was asked
When execution was near
Any last words? Switch

Candle

When the lights go out
And you want to set the mood
Light up a candle

Deliverance

When you are in pain
Pray…it may take some time, but
He will deliver

Massage

Relaxes your mind
Takes you to another world
It's therapeutic

www.ingramcontent.com/pod-product-compliance
Lightning Source LLC
Chambersburg PA
CBHW060041050426
42448CB00012B/3093